Jacob

THE
RAMBLINGS
OF MY
MADNE22

www.justanordinarybloke.com

Other books in this series

www.justanordinarybloke.com

jacob

THE
RAMBLINGS
OF MY
MADNESS

Volume 2
BLOOD, TEARS AND INJUSTICE

ISBN 978-0-99328-342-0

A catalogue record for this book is
available from the British Library.

Published by Outspoken Products Ltd.
Printed in the United Kingdom.
First printed in 2015 by BookPrintingUK.com.

For more copies of this book, please email:
jacob@justanordinarybloke.com

JAcOB
PO Box 516
Farnborough
GU14 4GR

www.justanordinarybloke.com

To my **brother** and **sister**

Thank you for being a **safety line**
in my life and for being there
through it all.

With all my **love**,

Bruv

SPECIAL THANKS

Inspiration for the content of this book has come in the strangest ways.

The volume that you are reading today, in its current form, is the result of the dedication and hard work of two very special and talented people. The journey that these two dear friends have undertaken, in the giving of such unwavering support, is extraordinary.

Without their love, friendship, honesty and compassion, this project would quite simply never have happened. I really know not of words to thank you both for such a beautiful gift.

Thank you so very, very much.

With love,

CONTENTS

BLOOD, TEARS AND INJUSTICE | 12

POETRY | 16

BLOOD, TEARS AND INJUSTICE

Since landing back on England's green and pleasant land, I've struggled to find meaning to carry on living.

Re-integration into a normal existence has been harder than I thought, not that I had any concious expectations of myself. I've been working as much as I can and, almost immediately on my return, I seemed to be making headway with generating business.

What little undefinable will I had to want to live though has been kicked out of me by the ugly reality of injustice, greed, gluttony and the sinister ways of some of mankind.

I received a long affidavit from the Canadian court, which I wasn't even able to read, followed by yet another judgment on my failings as a father and moreover as a human being.

Numerous attempts at trying to get legal help in the UK appear wasted.

In eight years of ups and downs, I've never resorted back to smoking and drinking in volume. My exercise has usually been consistent and daily, yet, in the weeks since my return to England, I find no motivation to exercise and have started smoking and drinking again. I know this isn't the answer but this self-destruction is evidence of how depression can manifest itself.

For me, exercise has usually left me with a sense of wellbeing and I understand this isn't the case for everyone, but I have historically used exercise in my fight against depression.

For now, I conclude, if I were diagnosed with an imminent terminal disease, I might well take the actions that I have previously comtemplated and would most likely feel a sense of relief. Currently, I see no reason and have no desire for an elongation of existence. For me, the loss of my daughters, possibly forever, is equivalent to a terminal diagnosis. On top of this manifestation, the abuse meted out by the idiots in the Canadian justice system, the careless nature of the British court system, dealing with depression itself, fighting tooth and nail to keep a business alive for such a long time now and, of course, being in constant physical pain feels just too much to bear; though by far, the greatest pain I feel, as always, is emotional. I miss my daughters.

There have been many judgements made of me and my actions and some of those are completely justified.

For I have made a plenitude of mistakes and blunders in my life as a result of my stupidity, lack of foresight, depression (a statement of fact rather than an excuse) and, in some case, just my attempts at doing the best I can.

I have also been judged at the hands of the so-called 'justice' system in Canada. I feel that these are heinous, arrogant and ignorant, and come from people to which ordinary folks look to for fairness to prevail. It is my feeling that this judge, who has conveniently turned away from asking questions that would have forced her into a line of action for which courage would be required, has failed her title, her responsibility, herself, my daughters and me.

Presiding over the case, she publicly declared, "If it's a choice between the children having a father or money, they get the money.".

This woman carries a title in front of her name for which I feel she is not fit. However, even more disturbing is the woman who has had a substantial part to play in promoting and provoking such judgements with her lies.

Further disturbance, in my own personal experience and that of many other folks, is that the losers are innocent young children who are denied a family in some manner or other.

And again, let's be clear here, I am not blameless. I have made lots of big mistakes in my life; however, the sentencing does not match the crime by a country mile.

POETRY

1.
IT'S BEEN A LONG TIME

It's been a long time,
    The **relativity** sublime,
The fights we fought
    Left each other distraught.

And, even though 10 years has passed,
    There's no end in view or **finish** at last,
So what of living in the here and now?
    Maybe I'll Google it to find out how.

But of this thing called self I'm learning,
    Is the **tide** inside finally turning?
Has it taken 49 years for me to learn
    That which others can in a term?

All the questions that **spin** and more,
    Most end up smashed on the floor.
And though I use poetry to express,
    I don't deny, I've caused a mess.

And so, I revisit the hooded claw,
    Not love, the one called the law,
But she ain't **justice** no more,
    She's just a title, fit for the garbage door.

So as not to be distracted,
    I come back, to the ways I've acted
And of what I **contemplate** now.
    Am I about to jump or bow?

Talking in the third, I've heard,
    Opens expression to word,
So on another day, I will say
    Save your love for another day.

2.
TIME

Time seems to have passed,
    How **long** will this last?
An eternity defined
    By sun shone, now shined.

Grains of sand,
    Lifted from the earth,
Held up to the sky,
    Slip from **worth**.
I know that I live in a bubble,
    I have made folks **miserable**
With my insensitive waxing
    And drinking and smoking.

Break my heart if you must,
    I suppose that's only just,
It's about time I had a **taste**,
    Of the bitter winds that paste.

My friend says, in desperate tone,
    Listening to an **empty** phone,
I look at pictures of past
    And I know it cannot last.

Perhaps I should let go now,
Is my breathing an act of **selfishness**?
If you can hear this,
Please guide me out of this.

3.
TODAY

Today, it **hurts** more than other days,
    I remembered some of your little ways.
Today, I **wander** through the mall,
    Looking in the stores you used to.

Today, is just a relative **reaction**
    To missing you both and that interaction,
It's not right that you're being **kept** from me,
    Didn't I always do my best for thee?

Today, I'm aware that you're still young,
    I've made **mistakes** and come undone,
Of these things, I'm well aware
    But I'm still your Daddy, to be **fair**.

Today, you're both somewhere,
    Is it right I know not **where**?
I send a message to you every day,
    Invariably, it seems, they go **astray**.

Today, I'm **aware** it's not your fault,
    But, when you're older, you'll halt
For a moment or two, and **remember**
    The many good times, not that sad December.

Today, I know I'm far from **perfect**,
　　When you get older you'll both reflect,
When you realise you're imperfect too
　　And that, **irrespective**, I love both of you.

Today, I thought of the pancakes I made
　　With **love**, for you both, when you stayed,
And of the sleepovers, and the **caring** thought
　　That went into my time with you, as ought.

Today, I'm **grateful** for the times I've tried,
　　Sometimes it feels like you've both died,
Without **word**, I feel like you've both passed on,
　　One day you'll read this, maybe when I'm gone.

Today, I drink my **memories** of us,
　　The excitement of riding that school bus,
The **novelty** of being on that street car,
　　The train, the plane, on which we journeyed far.

Tonight, as I turn out my light,
　　Your **stars** will, in my heart, shine bright,
Simply, I can rest and be at peace,
　　I've done my best, for to **release**.

Tonight, I will close another suitcase,
　　Full of my **thoughts** of your trace,
You'll move on, and I'll not know where
　　And that's the **sad** reality for you pair.

Tonight, I'm still your Daddy
   And as sun sets, I'll pray you're **happy**,
You'll need this in times to come,
   Heartache, like that **splinter** in your thumb.

Tomorrow, that **dagger** in my heart,
   The longer we're apart,
Will ache and **smart** a little less,
   At peace, I know I did my best.

Tomorrow, like the last hundred days,
   I'll send a **message** of love, of your ways
I'll know not, whether this love greets you,
   For **silence** is what I expect, to be true.

Tomorrow, I'll remind myself you're still small,
   And **hope** you'll know soon, it's good to call,
For I'm still you're Daddy, you know,
   A long, long way from **perfect** I am, I know.

4.
CANADA

The **wind** that howls, the **snow** does drive,
   The freezing **rain**, upon my face, does writhe
And bruises my soul and very being,
   Enough of this place for
   100 lifetimes I've been seeing.

But of this place I must **hide** my face,
   Or at least the way I'm feeling,
For 'tis my daughters' **home**,
   And this is where their souls will roam.

The **justice** system wreaks,
   The judges are all freaks,
Lawyers, like the bleeding leach,
   Keep a father **out of reach**.

This place, of course, is not all bad
   Yet, a gut-full of tripe from here I've had,
It's nigh on **impossible** to be heard,
   A loving father, an extinct bird.

There is **no fairness** in this place,
   So guard, from freezing rain, your face.
It's more important to **get the money**,
   Than for a daughter to have a loving Daddy.

So Canada, I bid you, up your arse!
   The court system's a frigging **farce**,
Go and eat yourself to an early grave,
   Here's one bloke who, on that day, will rave.

There are some **good souls** here,
   And for those fine folks, I care so dear,
But, God knows, those fine are rare,
   Go stuff yourself with processed fare.

Canada, a land where **opportunity** knocks
   For the unemployed, greasy, fat cocks.
They **preach** of love and all that crap,
   Yet look at them, with pizza on their lap.

Their inherent self-abuse must be
   A deep-seated **unhappiness**, you see,
For why on earth would you
   Do what you do?

But one day, mark my words,
   A black crow from Hitchcock's band
Upon your shoulder will land,
   As **penance** for lazy hand.

And hail you descendant to Hell,
   The truth will **ultimately** tell
You are no better than any of us,
   You fat lazy useless ass.

5.
THE HURT INSIDE

I've felt the depths of **despair**,
    And felt sick to my soul.
I've felt **broken** and burnt
    And black as night, black as coal.

I've felt **kicked** to my core,
    With this hurt so raw,
As I've **strained** to hold on,
    But times come, and I must be gone.

I can't **escape** the imagery
    Of you treating yourself so cheaply.
I'm feeling the **hurt** inside,
    And the tsunami of sadness tide.

I can't even begin to **reconcile**,
    I wish I could, I wish I could smile,
You say it's not who you are today,
    But that's **not right** any which way.

It's like I've been **punched** and **winded**,
    The morning after this has not rescinded.
I wish I could turn these **emotions** off,
    And hold your heart high aloft.

Away from the many hands they've **mauled**
And **violated** and used your all,
The nausea does not abate,
It's as if poison I ate.

I know we all have history
And I'm **scared** now, of what I'll see
When in your eyes I longingly look,
Will it be your past or those who took?

I wept in the shower this morning,
As reality of this **sadness** was dawning.
I wept as much for you as I did for myself,
All that's left is to wish you good health.

I know you're a good and beautiful soul,
Truth is, I'm a simple man, and that's the whole.
Yes, I've been visited by the **damned**
And their fists, into my heart, have **slammed**.

I will sit with **darkness**, my old friend,
And my beaten heart will slowly mend.
It's no one's fault, I am who I am,
While in **pain**, I'm at peace with who I am.

I can barely believe that my angel has **gone**,
Upon my brow your light has shone,
My eyes **burned** and now I'm blind,
So, alone I'll be, to rest my heart and mind.

6.
ODE TO LIGHT

I've weaved a **life** that has brought me to peace,
 But don't think that I've not cried for release,
Many roads have I walked and **searched**,
 Many times I've stumbled and lurched.

Yes, this life here is a **destination**,
 But it's also just an urban station
On the track that this tram **travels**,
 A route that eventually unravels.

And pass, as those ships do, in the dead of night,
 Warn us, with a **beacon**, lest we lose sight,
Hold your heart open and be real to yourself,
 Follow your heart, and **breathe** good health.

The **message** here is an ode to light,
 For with light, dark is banished from sight,
With love, there can be nothing less,
 In peace I come, bearing **kindness**.

7.
IF I LOVED YOU

If I loved you,
   Would I **stand** and watch you get manipulated?
If I loved you,
   Would I **watch** your beliefs get derated?
If I loved you,
   But felt **differently**, should I walk away?
And if I love you,
   Wouldn I not **wish** you well on your way?

For in loving you and holding so dear,
   I feel **angst**, when I'm not near
To face the challenges we face,
   While we live in a different place.

I talk of thoughts that consume,
   Of feelings that **fester** in vacuum,
Trashy talk of what you hold dear,
   Some of which seem very clear.

So if I love, would I not let you be
   And slip away ever so **silently**?
And as I hang on, feeling deflated,
   Perhaps it's me that's outdated.

Yet, be that the case or not,
  Mistakes I've made, many and lot,
With or without you, I'm just the same
  Though **together**,
  I'd prefer in heart and name,
But as I've mused in recent hour,
  Agreements are easy and bear **flower**,
But, through challenge, we really grow,
  Be that together, or apart, I do not know.

Of course, this is all just rhetoric,
  All I know is I feel sick,
On the edge of desperation, once again,
  As these words flow from my **electric** pen.

Can I accept the ridiculousness of fact?
  Can I let this be and turn my back?
Can I **simply** live and let live?
  Can I do all this and still of my soul give?

A shallow and simple man I must be,
  For I cannot watch this injustice I see
And not seek to offer **perspective**,
  For us, I simply want to love and live.

Do we really need anyone to show us what's right?
  Surely, for ourselves, we can see dark and light?
I can't **embrace** or bear the bitter taste
  Of my beautiful girl, exploited and laced.

So, with deep breath and teeth gnashing,
   I share this **honesty** and bear the lashing,
With a cat of nine tails I feel whipped,
   In fact, I'd rather this
   Than the untruth on which I've tripped.

8.
REST IN YOUR DREAMS

Dear child, dear daughters of mine,
    Rest in your dreams in the **sunshine**,
Dear daughter, dear daughter, you gifts from God,
    Thankyou for your love so **pure**,
    Your love so fine.

Rest in your dreams as you close your eyes,
    Rest, till you wake **peacefully** at sunrise,
Ready and eager to live another day,
    Ready and **excited** to laugh and play.

Dear children, dear daughters, so unique,
    You're in my **heart** every day, every week,
Close your eyes as you rest this night,
    And when morning comes when day is **bright**.

Rest in your dreams as you lay still in bed,
    Rest, till you **wake** to see the day ahead,
With curious abandonment, forwards you tread,
    The nighttime comes again,
    And I **settle** you in bed.

God bless you both my **angels** of hope,
    Rest in your dreams, wake in your hopes,
Ready to **share** your discoveries of this day,
    And bring awareness to those jaded today.

9.
PARTS OF MY SOUL

For a whole long time now,
   I've asked all these **questions**.
Did you ever think about
   Who made those **suggestions**?
I don't know how long I'm going to be here,
   None of us know, so why **fear**?
But, as I stand beside you, hand on your shoulder,
   As I hold you close to me, time makes me **older**.

For a whole long time now, I've worried about you.
   Did I ever think about who led me to you?
And it matters not how long I'm going to be here,
   I say this to you for when I'm gone and not near.

Stand tall, stand **proud**,
   Sing for me, sing clear, sing **loud**,
Look in that mirror and smile,
   You'll see me if you wait a while.

For longer than I care to think, I've searched inside.
   Did I ever listen to my heart, or in myself confide?
I've **hurt** you, I've **cursed** you,
   And you know I meant it too.
But the parts of my soul, the object of my love,
   They're the ones I've **attacked**,
   From high above,
I miss you all, the parts of my soul, with all my love.

The Ramblings of my Madness - Volume 2 - Blood, Tears and Injustice

10.
THE FOOL I'VE BEEN

Just like **seeing** is believing,
    The feeling is shown in the **doing**,
And, much the same as the dawn rise,
    The **truth** I see is in your eyes.

It's there to see, no mistaking,
    The fool I've been **trusting**, my **feeling**,
While I live just day to day,
    You don't want to **hear** what I have to say.

So, I'll just keep these thoughts to **myself**,
    I'll plan my death and you plan your wealth,
And to the **onlooker**, all will be fine,
    Except to say, the final truth is mine.

The notes I've left, the things I've said,
    They say it all, I'm **broke** in my head.
It's different now to what it was before,
    I have no will, or want, to fight anymore.

So I'll just keep it all **hidden** inside,
    I did my best, Lord knows I tried,
OK, maybe it simply wasn't good enough,
    But I'm not that strong, I'm not that tough.

There's no map to navigate this cloud,
    The May tree **blooms** as I think aloud,
Writing in riddles, thinking in rhymes,
    Wondering what's next, more **troubled** times.

So I'm moving on to another place,
    In daydreams of darkness, there'll be no **trace**.
I'll **exit** quietly and close the door,
    Leave the room tidy, and return no more.

11.
THE DECK

One by one, the deck of **cards** fell,
 Through the months, the **cracks** did tell,
Long before any **corners** were turned,
 In the **fire** of love, we both got burned.

We both seemed to **lose** our way,
 There's **nothing** more that I can say,
Though we tried and tried and tried to stay
 True to our **promises**, true to our way.

And now we live apart each day
 From the hurt we caused along the way,
We both played a **role** in this war,
 And now I wonder what was it for?

One by one, the deck of cards will **rise**,
 Time will continue to separate ties
And **good riddance** to you, thunder thighs!
 I'll eat salad, you go eat pies!

One by one, the days go by,
 Sometimes I wonder why
Your ship in the night did pass by,
 All I know is, I did try.

12.
BETTER

Better, to have had love and to lose
   When you look back and feel used.
Better, to feel taken for granted
   Than to hear "what if ..." chanted.

Better, to be reminiscent of the past
   When you see the lover last
Than to wonder what may have been,
   At least you can say that you've seen.

Better, to be kissed and felt touch,
   Even though I miss you so much,
The river of time runs fast,
   I keep looking for a love to last.

Better, to have much to learn
   And to know of what you yearn.
Better, to be alone with hope of happiness
   Than to be in with no awareness.

Better, to think of you each day,
   The river slowly washes away
The scars we left with each other,
   And grasp that which we shared together.

Better, to feel grateful for our time,
    And to have watched each hour chime
In darkness, till the light bleeds through,
    And to still feel the cold of missing you.

Better, to lie on a cold stone floor,
    Secrets of continuance, before
Slowly the weeping wound is stitched,
    And our hearts become unhitched.

But better, by far, all this
    And to know the hopeful wish,
And to have our hopes dashed,
    To feel beaten and thrashed,
Than to wonder, or turn away,
    For the river that runs this day
Will run forever, whatever we say,
    Believe in yourself and your way.

13.
WOUND UP SO TIGHT

Even as I tried to kiss you in your sleep,
  Even then, you were **wound up** so deep,
Can't bring yourself to respond to a kiss,
  So, tell me please, what on earth is this?

A man can only take so much **knocking back**
  Before that harvest moon fades dull to black,
Bound up by your own expectations,
  Wound up by your human limitations.

Goodness me, such **overt hostility**,
  Thank goodness the end came quickly.
I'm walking away, but I do wish you well,
  Perhaps peace will deliver you
  From your personal Hell?
You **can't control** others, I know you know,
  You can only choose what you feel
  And what you show,
It's not time to get knee-deep in shit,
  But let the peace of love upon you hit.

It's not always because of **sub-agenda**,
  But more because of the love
  You've stretched tender,
There are mostly good folk in this worldly place,
  Sure, mistakes we all make but offer some grace.

You **didn't understand** my love,
Maybe you've been burned,
   Yet belief of fair hand,
   My love was beside and yearned,
No matter now 'Jelly Bean', I wish you well,
   Toward the sun do lean, and then go tell.

14.
COBALT BLUE

Cobalt blue and green,
   Were these the shades you'd seen?

Without hesitation,
You went where few dared to go,
   A leader, a lover,
   And courage like we never know,
The garden you planted flourishes still
   And in our hearts you will remain until.

Bathe and rest your weary hands,
   For when we meet again on golden sands
And walk together, like times gone by,
   You showed us in our dreams we all can fly.

You never gave up the good fight,
   You fought with all your heart,
In darkness you shone your loving light,
   You stilled many a stormy night.

Cobalt blue and green,
   Was this the sky you'd seen?

You once talked of colours you could not describe,
 You'd seen these shades
 When you journeyed to the other side,
From the darkness of despair you rose
 And through us all, your spirit grows.

And the gift you gave of love and grace
 Is how I'll remember the smile on your face,
By example, you taught many things,
 When I look above I hear angels sing.

You broke your silence in defence,
 You stood for those alone,
You shone a beacon to guide us home,
 Now you're gone from skin and bone.

Cobalt blue and green,
 Was this where you'd been?

I was lost, when I thought you'd left,
 But now I realise you never went,
Your body was just to your spirit lent,
 And now I know you were heaven-sent.

Cobalt blue and green,
 Is this the place you'd been?

And now I write these words and so many more,
 The question, "What was it all for?",
Simply needs no answer anymore,
 For your being here still, of that I'm sure.

In darkness you did battle
With the demons at your door,
    Like the champion you are you triumphed before,
A flag-bearer for truth, a light of grace,
    Your light burned the darkness and left no trace.

You broke rank and file,
    As you ground out mile after mile,
In stoic belligerence
    Of your body's ill deliverance.

Cobalt blue sky you'd seen,
    Green meadows of velveteen,
This is where you rest, between,
    With a view of satin sheen.

15.

A PHONE CALL TO THE BRIDGE

Just about a month ago,
    I took your **drawings** off the fridge,
Guess I'd like to let you know
    It's just a **phone call** to the bridge.

The drugs numb my senses
    Of **missing you** both so bad,
So many emails and **so few responses**,
    Maybe not hearing from me makes you glad?

So, maybe now it's time
For me to put your **photos** away,
    Just one at a time, to ease the pain of each day,
Truth be told, I know not what's for the best,
    And perhaps for me, this is just some test.

I know you're both still so young,
    And I find myself wondering
Things like, how you've had your **hair** done,
    Till I find myself surrendering.

I hope you learn much quicker than I,
    Before too much **time passes** by,
That you are responsible for your choices,
    Irrespective of the present adult voices.

And, with this in mind, if this is it,
   Then I'll simply keep a **candle** lit,
One for each of you, in my heart
   For you will always be a part.

And now I must draw to a close,
   For too long has passed, as it goes,
The **ticking clock**, the hands have stopped,
   The chiming bell I know so well.

Telling me you did the best you could
   And I'd do it all again, I truly would,
Nope, there are no regrets here,
   Let those **vicious voices** rasp your ear.

For God alone will be my judge,
   And so, I'll send my love, with no taint or grudge.

16.
A THREAD OF LOVE

Sending lots of hugs
  To my two beautiful snuggle bugs,
Wishing upon many a star
  That you're happy, from afar.

Missing you lots and lots,
  Saving love for you both, in pots,
When you are ready and good,
  From a plane I'll jump, I would.

I think of you both everyday,
  I write songs I'll never play,
Some though I may record,
  Perhaps, one day, from where they're stored.

And, if the night should pass by,
  These will be left, for I did try
To keep a thread of love free for thee,
  So all I can wish is that you're happy.

17.
IF YOU LOVE SOMETHING

Not a day, barely an hour
  Passes, **sun** or shower,
Without missing you so,
  Another day and the star **shines** low.

It's said, if you **love** something, "Let it go"
  And if it comes back, you'll know
That love will **always** be yours,
  And if not, it never was.

Barely a minute, not even a breath,
  From now to the **day** of my death,
Will the stars not know I love you so?
  Maybe a **month**,
  Maybe a **year**,
  Maybe never.

So I **send** you all the love I can,
  An English pancake in a pan
With Golden Syrup, and Daddy's love,
  Listen close to the **stars** above.

They **whisper** and hum,
  A familiar tune, tum, tum, tum,
Sending a big squishy hug
  To keep your beautiful **hearts** snug.

18.
IN YOUR TIME

In your time, in your time,
    Seeing you again.
In your time, in your time,
    Talking with you again.

In your time, in your time,
    Accepting what will be will be.
In your time, in your time,
    Wishing you well once again.
In your time, in your time,
    You may **call** again.
In your time, in your time,
    You will **lead**, should we walk again.

In your time, in your time,
    And should our paths **diverge**.
In your time, in your time,
    I pray that angels **guide** your way.

In your time, in your time,
    Thanks for the time we **shared** today,
In my time, in my time,
    You'll have my **well wishes** anyway.

19.
BEAST

The door was left open, so I thought I'd come inside,
    Welcome is not a word I'd use to confide,
Such a **parasite** that takes all there is to take,
    Finding happiness much harder to fake.

So come in if you must,
I have **no choice** to make,
    You'll come and you'll take all you can take,
But, with heavy heart, mine will be the final stake,
    For when I jump,
    I'll take my friend to meet the Corncrake.

Beautiful is not a word I'd use to describe,
    Desperate is how you **leave me** feeling inside,
So hang on tight, you peculiar friend,
    Come with me on this last flight to the end.

Yes beast, beast, go away,
    Don't, I dare you come another day,
Stay if you like but be prepared, for **I will fight**
    For with you I will go, and fly from high bow.

Yes, the beast that bites fulfils its appetite
    By **tearing flesh** from my soul,
But, I'm alive and alone,
    But, I'm alive and atoned.

20.
MIRRORS AND MEMORIES

Picture your life in a thousand shards,
    Imagine that's all there is, it's hard,
The edges are **sharp** and cut you raw,
    Till all you can do is shut the door.

Broken mirrors and broken memories,
    Any good **severed** by misery,
Time and again there's someone to blame,
    But perhaps, in truth, it's all in my name.

And so, to decide and make a choice
    Is not so hard, and **clear** is the voice
As I mutter beneath my final breath,
    I'll open the door and welcome death.

To all those I love, every one of you,
    Justly, you would do what is **right** for you,
I love you all and always will,
    And we'll be together again so, until ...

Breathe the **early** morning air,
    Touch the face of an angel,
Savour the taste
    Of sunshine on your face.

Hold the hand of a **dying** friend,
    For nigh is the end,
And know these things are all blessings,
    This is life with all the dressings.

21.
FAIL

Thinking of the passage of time,
    Feeling sad that actions don't rhyme,
This life into insignificance does pale
    When darkness falls and I fail.

22.
WHERE I'M STANDING

I'm not sure where I'm standing anymore,
   It's like the black light, through a familiar door,
Beckons me with promise to an end of pain,
   For even on sunny days, my world is full of rain.

There's a feeling of peace,
   As I consider release,
I'm breathing air,
   From somewhere.

Comfortably numb,
   Hearing distant drum,
A walk to my tree,
   And goodbye to thee.

23.
NO GOING BACK

When there's **nothing left** to say,
  When it can't be heard any other way,
When there is just **one path** ahead,
  And going back fills you full of dread.

When this time is upon you,
  Pack away, and **leave tidy** too,
Leave the notes you've prepared,
  And **bid farewell** to those who cared.

To many this will seem a **selfish act**,
  And perhaps that's the truth and fact,
But consider, for a moment, and you may see
  A Daddy, lost to his daughters, **setting free**.

Folk may talk of obligation,
  But with peace, I believe expectation
Is not a fair card to play,
  For my daughters must go their **own way**.

24.
GOING TO AMERICA

Loneliness is a strange kind of friend,
 Reflection of the past till the **end**.
The bartender calls time,
 Are we at the end of the line?

Seems there's many a place like here,
 Places where **life** has left, that's clear.
Towns run dry of spirit and beer,
 Bars where there's no talk or cheer.

Looking deep into a frosted glass,
 There's time to stare into the **past**.
Climbing up on rock to scene,
 The Shenandoah Valley green.

I might as well be waffling away,
 There's not an awful lot to say,
Except to ask where to buy a gun
 And let the churning **extinguish** my sun.

A beauty beside my soul
 Has left me half, not whole,
For without you in my life,
 There's no point in the **strife**.

So screw me over again and again,
  It won't be long now till the end.
Bring the curtain down right now,
  I've taken my **final bow**.

Of course, it's all just about rambles,
  But God knows it's a flaming shambles.
Justice is a **miscarriage** of words,
  An elk strayed from the herds.

Wandering **alone** on a path,
  There ain't a chance, not even half,
That the tide may turn
  So die, you scorned, and in Hell may you burn.

But back to the roadhouse,
  And big country inn,
The long winding road,
  And the **suffering**.

It's a life away from home,
  To turn your back and be alone.
Duane Allman and those guys,
  With talk of a **new sunrise**.

Two down and a few to go,
  Up and down and more you know.
Isn't it **time yet**, or near,
  That my dear daughters will be clear?

For themselves, a life and a way,
    I love you both, what did you do today?
Did I even enter your mind?
    It's OK if not,
    One day these **thoughts** you'll find.

Strangely feels that I'm getting closer to who I am,
    Belief in loss and that endless tram.
I've made my mistakes and can't **deny**,
    And I wouldn't even bother to try.

You see, I'm not ashamed one little bit,
    I did my best to keep that candle lit,
But, about my love for you two,
    There's not a flame brighter, that's **true**.

And as this night sneaks in,
    I'll hold you **deep within**.
You see a Daddy's love is straight,
    Before it's dead, before it's too late.

And one by one, the number's dialled
    And a simple dad's love gets defiled.
And who's the real bearer of this **wrath**?
    The children left, a different path.

But sooner or later, the winds will blow
    And the **autumn colours** will show,
Before you lift another limb,
    You fat sloth and belly brow Jim.

INTERLUDE

I've only lived 49 years, but some would say I've lived several lives already. That's not a reference to reincarnation; it's simply about my experiences.

Now don't be mistaken, I've always said I am just an ordinary bloke and I maintain that. In fact, I'm a very ordinary bloke who has made the most incredible blunders and mistakes, some funny, some downright irritating, and many that have caused myself and my loved ones huge distress.

When I was about 25, I jumped out of an aeroplane and I think ever since that day, through my many ups and downs, I've had this feeling that if I die this day then that's ok.

I've done lots of things, good and bad, but I believe in my heart I've done the best I could. Some folks may contest this.

There is something about the injustice I've experienced that makes it hard to stand still and be at home for too long. For this reason I travel, and 'The Ramblings of My Madness - Volume 3 - Different Time, Different Place' reflects on this further.

During my time in America, I'd been doing a lot of walking; Mary's Rock, Humpback Rock (near Waynesboro), Sharp Top Trail and Rocky Knob, whilst staying in Floyd.

Rock Castle Gorge at mile marker 167.1 was a good hike. I got lost, but managed to recover a potentially hazardous situation.

After losing my bearings and the sun going down much quicker than I thought, I was in the bottom of a gulley about 400ft deep, so there was nothing to take bearings from.

I cut a limb from a tree with my wire saw and used it to climb out of the gulley to a point where I could again see the sun and take bearings and eventually got back to safety.

Down in the Smokies I climbed Monte Le Conte, about 18 miles round trip and an elevation of about 2600ft.

It was cold and icy and I felt there were eyes on me for a lot of the way ... bears. They were very nearby and, although I never got a clear sighting, I did come across bear droppings which were still warm.

Having been away for 11 days, I started to ask myself, "What are you looking for?". Retrospectively speaking, this was a big shift in my state of mind that day.

In Atlanta airport, going back to the UK for a few days just to see my nearest and dearest, I did some more reflection ...

MORE POETRY

25.
BROTHERS AND SISTERS

The love you've shown forces me to pause,
    Before I manifest the final cause,
A bucket list to stave off hunger,
    A distraction break, away my anger,
Money will buy me time, that's true,
    You, right now, I'm just too tired to see,
Ahead, above the deep dark cloud,
    Is a simple cry, yet not so loud.

You guys have left me feeling sad,
    For I love you all and hear your call,
I feel your love in my heart, I do,
    So how can I survive this misery too?
My heart hurts and is tired of justice,
    Seems the judge is blind and mindless
From the reality of fact,
    Guess to them I'm just an act.

But their kind of justice is farcical.

26.
THE HIGHWAY AHEAD

The life ahead provides many a choice,
   The highway, at each fork,
   Will **whisper** a voice
To quiet the mind, so listen well
   And maybe then a **tale** to tell.
Of the highway we've travelled,
   The tangled ball is unravelled,
Where we find a place that's right,
   No longer a need to fight.

Perhaps of naïve Utopia I dream,
   But beside a dream goes desire to seam
And to sow a path with a **kindred** soul,
   Hand in hand, both us who we are.
I've often fallen short, by far,
   Of the man I hoped I would be,
But peace in **hindsight** is me.

So the road this very day
   I will choose to come your way,
Many things I will feel and that's OK
   You see, at peace I am with me,
And whosoever you may be,
   A coffee, a beer, a shot or three,
It matters not if our **journeys** align,
   For if it's to be, there will be a sign.

27.
1200 MILES

1200 miles I'd driven in **silence**,
  For to consider the justice laments,
They took my children,
  So what's left then?

A life, a **broken** heart, a shell,
  Emptiness of mind I know well,
Such a long way from perfect,
  My mistakes, proof of my defect.

1200 miles became a **whole** lot more,
  Running out of purpose to live for,
I was never blameless, that's for sure,
  Was I the only one wrong or was there more?

Justice **speaks**, and would rather
  The children have money than a father,
How does a person like you sleep at night?
  I'm empty and fault full, and you're all right.

Three thousand, six hundred miles
  And the judge opens the files,
Reads the smoke screen of **deception**,
  And therein finds reception.

A **convenient** conclusion to mute,
    She says the numbers didn't compute,
But does that mean it's all bullshit,
    The underlying facts of this murky pit?

Yes, a pit of honorary **injustice**
    Presided over by dismal miss Ziss,
You don't deserve the title Madame,
    Dismal is, as dismal done to them.

Cosset yourself in your grand black robes,
    Trip and break your **ignorant** nose,
Slip and come undone at the seams
    'Cos you've no longer got a brain between.

You ought be nailed to a two by four,
    Come and take a little more,
Protect yourself and your **twisted** law,
    Wait till the press hear this tale of yours.

You're a slight decency and humanity,
    You're beyond any kind of stupidity,
Still, we 'all rise'
Beyond our level of **incompetence**
    Congratulations! You've gone the distance.

28.
I SAW YOUR NAME IN THE SNOW

As I trod with respect on virgin snow,
    And marvelled at the valley below,
As I bent into the bracing chill,
    I noticed a **warmness** fill.

I saw your name in the snow,
    Of course I wrote it just so,
And in my mind you were there,
    Never above, never below, just there.

I retraced my steps down,
    Heading back to the **bustling** town,
People going about their business,
    Almost too busy to dismiss.

And then, I saw your name in the snow
    With a kiss placed carefully below,
And in a photo I tried to embrace
    The feelings I had, **recalling** your face.

29.
IT'S ALL IN THE TITLE

It's all in the title,
    Everything and nothing at all,
Climbing mountains out of season
    To try and discover reason.

I've felt comfort and peace,
    Seen grandeur and grace,
Brilliance embrace,
    Danger and disgrace.

Been at the pulpit of precipice,
    Felt friendship and injustice,
Wondered for native folks' heritage,
    Here, hangover and remedy
    Come in one package.

30.
IT WAS NICE OF YOU TO SAY

Well, it was nice of you to say
    It's **no surprise** you're alone anyway,
How can you look in the mirror
    And **bawdily** bid good cheer?

You're the epitome of **bad manners**,
    Of ignorance and dirty spanners,
Yep, a greasy slime ball of **disingenuity**,
    Offering blessings of what exactly?

You pronounce honesty and disclosure,
    Yet you **can't handle** the truth, can ya?
A peace of mind may come to you one day,
    But until you see the **error** of your way ...

Nashville here I come, because of you,
    Yet you **blindly** ignore respect, don't you?
Go your way and don't think, go blind,
    The immature games of your **ignorant** mind.

31.
BEHOLDEN

Beholden is such a sorry theme,
    Still undone, I'm so at the seam,
For to love you both I truly do,
    Maybe you'll forget your Daddy, who
Loved you and did his level best,
    But I fear it's too late now,
Famine of a father's love,
    You'll not know, but he above.
One day to the stars you'll gaze,
    Perhaps as grown women for days,
As ugly as I am or was,
    I loved you simply because.
All I ever wanted for you
    Was the best, and I tried too,
But the louder frequent voices
    Will whisper of many choices,
And mistakes I made aplenty,
    Will you ever know what you meant to me?
One day, as parents, you may know
    Of the things I write and did show.

32.
THE BIG SLEEP

Sitting alone in another bar,
    Hearing my children from **afar**,
A little girl with red hair
    Reminds me of for whom I **care**.

Sitting in this bar to numb me,
    Thinking of my **Princesses**,
My big girl, lovely Berry,
    You know I miss you very.

Light another cigarette,
    Sip another beer, to get
Anaesthesia from my **memory of you**,
    Here in the land of the music blue.

Donna sings of hot love,
    Gone now like the Memphis glove,
No hills to climb here,
    Nothing to **distract** my tear.

You gotta know, I'm gonna go
    But in my poetry, you'll know,
Because there's nothing to calm
    My heart, to save you from **harm**.

The maker made his mark,
    Just a dog bites a bark
And it's **cut me** so deep,
    I gotta go to the Big Sleep.

33.
STANDING ON THE BALCONY

I have this growing fascination,
    Would the bough **hold** under tension?
Would I be able to get a sling to hold?
    Can the map finally **unfold**?

Standing on this balcony, night after night,
    Each day brings an **awakening** sight
Of injustice and unfairness,
    That's **no complaint**, just a passing kiss.

I see myself, bloodied and swinging,
    In this picture there is **no singing**,
I fantasise about going back to Africa,
    But there's **no good** I can do there.

I spill my thoughts on these pages,
    While she's alive, my body **rages**,
I contemplate writing her
    But she ain't **worth** the time to offer.

I'd have used the money to try and get well,
    I **failed** to mention that in court, oh well,
Can't bring myself to re-read the **judging** court
    So I think in Colorado, a gun can be bought.

Maybe it's best for everyone that this be done,
   I've **sunk** to my chest in drift and sun,
Thought a few times, the time has come,
   Still I came down, before the **storm** hum.

No swinging, no singing,
   No end and no bringing,
No peace, no release,
   No end and no more can I bend.

34.
I TRIED MY BEST

I tried my best,
    Seems I failed the test,
Those in gowns
    Are all court clowns.

I tried my best,
    Laughter and jest,
Parties and sleepovers,
    Christmases and Passovers.

I tried my best,
    Seems I'm just a pest,
The girls don't love me anymore,
    Of that, it seems, I'm sure.

I tried my best,
    Fun and all the rest,
Simply fell short of the mark,
    And now eternity in dark.

I prayed to God,
    A prayer so odd,
To take my life please,
    So sorry Lord, asking to ease.

I tried my best,
    Time may attest
To the failure I was,
    Trying because.

I tried my best,
    Yet all I did messed,
The efforts coming forth
    So I guess I'll head north.

I loved you so,
    And tried to show,
Was proud and told you so,
    But had to go slow.

I tried my best,
    Alone now, lest
A miracle should strike,
    And I fall on a spike.

35.
CHILD OF MINE

Child of mine, light so fine,
  Time gone by, time is **nigh**,
Memories of our moments,
  Leaves me hurting, **intense**.

Those times have disappeared,
  The winds of life saw you **grow**
And they left me desolate,
  Will you know how **I loved you**?

If the sun sets on my soul,
  Fate has broken me **whole**,
So maybe you'll know if I die,
  And you'll know how **I did try**.

Sweet children of mine,
  For a brief time I saw you **shine**,
But then the storm broke,
  And left me with all I **spoke**.

I just wanted to be your Daddy,
  But you ignored me too **soon**,
And now there's no day,
  So, I must be **on my way**.

When the day comes and I die,
　　Will you know all that **went by**?
Not a moment was spared,
　　I gave you all I was, **I shared**.

I got so many signs wrong,
　　Never was much **good at song**,
Those harsh winter chills
　　Blew me **off the hills**.

Went back to where you were,
　　But you didn't want me **anymore**,
So all I could do is leave your
　　Town, city, country, **door**.

In my lifetime, it was hard
　　To know **what to do**,
I prayed and asked God
　　To help me be the **best I could**.

Seems I failed, seems I will again,
　　Themes and **memories**, then,
Is all there is in my heart,
　　As I raise this gun to **blow me apart**.

36.
WHERE'S GOD THEN?

Amongst the hills,
   In between the trees,
The bitter wind chills,
   I've been on my knees.

And the question I hear
   In that land, so barren,
Death brings no fear,
   Where's God then?

Dare you show your face?
   Brave the wind in this place,
It's said you're in us all,
   Why then do we fall?

So where are you?
   Have I misconstrued true?
Most probably so,
   As I wonder where to go.
Have you left behind
   A trail that I can find,
Or am I simply blind
   To you, and your kind.

It's about time to level,
    For thoughts of dying
Are in which I revel,
    I'm tired now of trying.

Alienation and insularity,
    Doing my best inadequately,
Your spokesman sits aloft,
    Dismal I am in this croft.

And, just like the sun will rise
    Each day before my eyes.
The star of light will fall,
    And bring an end to it all.

Low and behold, it appears again,
    And I find myself upon this train,
Heading to I don't know where,
    Guess I'll know when I get there.

37.
TURN

Just like the **tide** alters,
   An ordinary man falters,
But to have a **bridge** burned
   Is to wonder what you've learned.

And to be so exclusive,
   As if to be **allusive**,
Potency of emotion,
   I know well the **notion**.

Still, you so **rapidly** turn
   And you so rapidly burn,
Still, that's your **choice** I guess,
   No wonder you're friendless.

Turn you will on a pinpoint,
   Break a bough so to **disappoint**,
We all are fallible and imperfect,
   So who are you to publicly **dissect**?

Turn you did, and **grateful** I am,
   You showed a side of terse vitriolism,
Turn you have, and turned you'll stay,
   But **don't you dare** talk to me that way.

Turn, and burn, and **disregard**,
    And alone you'll stay,
I'm full of faults and wrongs,
    And you are **far** from any such songs.

Turn.

38.
CORNERS

Corners of rooms,
   Corners we turn,
Corners of streets,
   And what did I learn?

Biding my time, till heading home
   To face the same old mess, I suppose.
Am I changed from what I've known?
   No, no difference that I can discern.

So heading back from this place,
   I came here to end this disgrace,
With recent events I've even thought
   Of atrocities, that come to nought.

Arriving home on a Tuesday,
   Been feeling rather low,
Reminded of the girls today,
   And reminded of what I know.

Completely unaware and not sure,
   Being here, was this like being near?
Can't say for certain what for ...
   But it feels like leaving my girls so dear.

Wish I could discern that a corner I'd turned,
    But with a court finally adjourned,
And with my girls not wanting me,
    Have no idea of my purpose here clearly.

39.
THESE DAYS

Sometimes, it's hard to **discern**
   Between dreams and real concern,
For a moment, **hope** exists
   And then in a blink, it's gone.

These days, **in pain**, are blurred,
   Self-medicated speech is slurred,
But come morning dawn,
   Reality and injustice **spawn**.

These days leave me thinking,
   What's the point, I'm just **sinking**.
It's said, the hardest part of drowning
   Is to see your **life crowning**.

What's all this talk about unjust?
   You're only as good as **trust**,
And does all that really matter?
   The thin go bald and the fat get **fatter**.

Flick your ash into a can of beer,
   And give the finger to those who **cheer**,
Justice for a father is non-distinct,
   And the fact of that matter, **extinct**.

Another day lost in the haze,
    Beneath **reams** of paper chains,
May just as well lay down and die,
    'Cos all your facts are a **deceptive lie**.

So what'll it be?
    A **browbeaten** obscenity?
Wish a curse on the fat and mad,
    For bad is good, and good is bad.

It's all got mangled and twisted,
    A smoke screen and fisted,
A hope, **extinguished**,
    And praying for death revisited.

40.
WHEN I THINK OF ALL THESE THINGS

I remember the flowers that lined the stairs,
    I remember fairies that hung by angel hairs,
It hurts to know it was all for nothing,
    The birthdays, the parties, the turkey stuffing.

I remember the stove at which I stood,
    Preparing us healthy food,
With love, I wrote you every day
    To nourish your hearts, while you play.

The monthly trips and the felt tips,
    The chocolate from England, and those little slips
That I placed inside your lunchbox each day,
    To feed your heart, in some small way.

I built our house into a loving home,
    You were poisoned and left me alone.
I still think of the trouble and the pain
    And the lengths to which I went to maintain.

It happens to be she'd have kept me away,
    But I fought and fought and found a way,
Simply to be a part of your world,
    But imperfect I am, unlike many others.

You're both older now, still tender in age,
    But able to make a choice,
    Which you do each day,
Not an email, let alone a call,
    Months have passed and I've not heard at all.

My questions go unanswered and justice is a joke,
    They took my money,
    And with it, the heart of this bloke,
You two have stamped me into the ground
    And left the hounds baying around.

I remember our kitchen and the hall,
    Your bedrooms and the special stool,
The red, the blue and white,
    The lengths to which I had to fight.

Now, it's your choice, and I'm here still,
    But I don't know how long I can say I will,
For a life without you is no life at all,
    I guess this one is your call.

Wiser folk than I have said,
    Fear not the ground you tread,
They say hurt's a sign you're doing something right,
    True, perhaps, but have I saved fight?

Each day brings me sadness now,
    I distract myself somehow,
But I care not for my life, as it stands,
    When I remember your sweet little hands.

41.
THE DAY BEFORE

The day before,
The devastation **tore**
    A child from its father's arms.

The day before,
Faith was **no more**,
    Despite God's ancient law.

The day before,
Is all just a **pit of darkness**,
    And so damn senseless.

The day before,
A child **slept** with her family,
    Now alone, with tears for company.

The day before,
Was an **existence**
    With no future, and no presence.

The day before,
Terror broke our **hypnosis**,
    Life's rhapsody went amiss.

The day before,
We held **each other's hands**,
    But now we stand on slipping sands.

The day before,
I knew of the **evil** in the DRC,
    I wondered what was next for me.

The day before,
I jumped from that **ledge**,
    And before any pledge.

The day before,
The end of **innocence**
    Has now past long since.

The day before,
I learned of **human atrocity**,
    There is no memory.

The day before,
The day before,
    The day before.

The day before,
I can't **remember** anymore,
    And now it's all gone, forever, for sure.

42.
ALL IS FINE

All is fine, all is good,
    I'd break a plate if I could.
All is fine, and God is good,
    Hide your eyes if you would.

All is fine, and covered in blood,
    But hush for fear of the communist hood.
All is fine, and everything is good,
    If I had the balls then jump I would.

All is fine, and the children fed,
    Are you kidding me, are you dead?
All is fine, in your little bubble,
    Don't rock the peace or stir the trouble.

All is fine, because for you it is,
    You still disgust me after all this.
All is fine, but on a wider scale,
    Hungry mothers and babies trail.

All is fine, just ignore the facts,
    It's easy to believe CNN tracks.
All is fine, they'd have us think,
    You media clowns grotesquely stink.

All is fine, a perfect fit,
    That's what you want to hear, isn't it?
All is fine, so don't patronise,
    There's still sight in these eyes.

All is fine, and just as planned,
    But for the love of God how can you stand?
All is fine, on the easy road,
    Judge, your ignorance really showed.

All might be fine, where you are near,
    But all I hear is a dying dog in my ear,
Nameless to me, but loved once you see,
    And now left to cry its way out of here.

All is fine, for the blessed in the fold,
    But that ain't me you ought be told,
All is fine, and before this life gets old,
    It'd better be settled or be sold.

All is fine, you failed the test,
    But you know you did your best.
All is fine, to the ordinary Jack,
    I hope there ain't no coming back.

All is fine, and always will be,
    For it is written you see,
All is fine, but I am losing the will
    To carry on this treacherous ill.

All is fine, and all complete,
    All is just so and all is neat,
For this is the word of the high,
    From where I am nowhere nigh.

All is fine, and just as well it might
    For blind to facts is eye, mind, sight,
Belief in what you are told,
    But change is, before you're old.

All is fine in bereavement,
    All is good in displacement,
Driven by a last goal,
    To print these words of soul.

43.
2015

Two thousand and fifteen
　　Is a sorry drifteen,
From the dawn of two thousand and fourteen,
　　From where my eyes had been.

Not so very much has changed,
　　Yet life today, to others seems **rearranged**.
I will lie alone this night, as the last,
　　And a day will see **no change** from the past.

My children have asked
　　What caused the **past**,
And yet to see them, I now realise
　　That my life is fault full and I despise.

The questions they **rightly ask**,
　　Amidst their growing questions of past,
Still these matter not, till they deem to be
　　In a place where we can simply be.

My precious daughters, I made mistakes,
　　As you grow older you'll see **many breaks**,
You may see these as entirely my fault,
　　But **it takes two** to unlock this vault.

44.
THE SHADOW'S LAST CALL

The **shadow**'s last call
  Came, before an end to it all,
The **shadow**'s last parade
  Came, as I became unmade.

The **shadow**s in this room
  May seal this vault, this tomb,
The **shadow**s of disgust
  Will die if they must.

The **shadow**s of a man,
  Left in tatters, in a can,
The **shadow**s of what remains
  Leave no **shadow**, just grains.

The **shadow**s of stories told
  And, before I get too old,
May the **shadow**s wither away
  And find another home on their way.

The **shadow**s of broken peace,
  The darkness of final release,
The **shadow**s of just one soul
  Give shade to something whole.

Can this be right of the **shadow**,
  In darkness, in fallow?
Let the night wake tomorrow,
  And my **shadow** rise and follow.

The **shadow** leaves no trace
  At first, it would seem,
But for the lines on another's face,
  And that's the hardest place.

45.
AND GRAND IS THE OCEAN

I look into the mirror amid dampened light,
　　To places inside, **empty** despite,
For there's no essence and no sight,
　　For the **battle** fought left no fight.

I write not for attention,
　　Despite the bloody **detention**,
But for a searching of truth
　　Around this **edge** of roof.

So, I will write before next morn's light,
　　The sun will win the **darkness** fight
And **rise** once more into view,
　　As night cries its morning dew.

Tapping away at this **medium**,
　　I welcome the sorrowful tedium,
It's a kind of **grace**, amidst my eyes,
　　That today I'll sleep and tomorrow I'll rise.

Still, be not fooled, for angst uncooled,
　　I'm **broken** and loose unspooled,
Wind in the mainsail,
　　Tether the lines, for a **storm** is tall.

And grand is the ocean and simple this man,
    A **mountain** has broken me, and yet I stand,
So I'll sing if the music fills the band,
    And if not, then I'll **wither** in sand.

And that would be just fine
    You see, deep inside, the **star** doth shine,
So to death I'm drawn without fear,
    And **alone** I will quietly embrace a tear.

46.
CLIMB

I sent **a picture** for your choice,
   Hoping just to hear your voice,
Saying, "I love you" was all I meant,
   But these days come and go and backs get bent.

You picked **a marble** that caught your eye,
   I took two for my climb on mountain high
So I could remember you for when I fall,
   The tears burn for lost years, that's all.

So for **my children** I'll carry two marbles,
   And that's all I can do, don't expect any calls,
For a criminal and a ghost is what I am to you,
   I may not be here when the truth dawns for you.

And if **my torture** is to continue,
   All I'll have is memory of you,
And if I fall, you'll be on that mountain,
   As you've been before again and again.

I will leave **my voice** up there with majesty,
   And leave your voice and memory.
Could I ask you to forget me?
   Could I ask God to let fall and be?

People say, "How can you do this thing?",
    Many say, many care, many sad if I'm not there,
How can this be the **drought** and **dread**?
    How can the news be, "He's dead.".

At morning dawn I will walk to the hills,
    With **Christmas joys** your heart fills.
Could I lie down and stare at the stars one last time?
    Would it be OK for
"I love you" to be my **last line**?

And if I lay with broken body,
    My spirit torn and shoddy,
Tear and snatch the breath out of me,
    It's been done before, I guess I'm **ready**.

From down here it's hard to see,
    The **summit** somewhere above me,
Into the wild and into the **abyss**,
    The fading memories I miss.

And about the who and the why,
    Should I **dare** to even try?
What if the fail is a cry?
    The time for writing draws **nigh**.

So if **it's time** for me to go,
    Just say and I will do so,
And angels will guide your path,
    And I will be **ashes** in a mountain hearth.

Ships that pass by this and every night
   Rarely do so **silent** in plight.
Can it be my daughters are now such?
   Your boat swept by **tide** so much.

47.
DEAR

Dear sun, where did you go?
  It was just an hour ago
I felt the warmth of your embrace,
  Now I can't even see your face.

Dear day, I feel you slipping away,
  There's nought I can do or say
To stop your waning light,
  Crowded out by this night.

Dear daughters, do you care?
  Dad's going to someplace, somewhere,
To replace your memory,
  With folk of sad story.

Dear life, dear breath, what on earth
  Was your intent and its worth?
The who you are,
  And are we far?

Dear night, now you're here
  And the dusk falls with fear,
Numb my senses and drug my pain
  And let this life from me drain.

48.
DAUGHTERS

Two daughters gone now,
   And no way somehow,
But if he could hold you,
   There might be a **future** too.

Two dear young souls gone,
   And what exactly has he done?
He fought and lost his **fight**
   Simply to be what a Dad might.

Now he sits, with paper and pen,
   Thinking of the now and the then,
But he has **fading** recall
   About being a Dad at all.

He built a home, **full** with love,
   A distant memory now departs above,
A home, made for his girls' dreams,
   Stolen by an evil bitch, it seems.

A place that is gone now,
   And no way back somehow,
Time is passing by as he writes,
   The battle **fought** and no more fights.

He lies down with a gun in his hand,
  Time slips by like grains of sand,
Two daughters gone now, may as well be **dead**,
  Gun in hand he buries the bullet in his head.

Yes he thinks he's lost here,
  Split in two by poisoned **spear**,
He thinks this is the end,
  His soul splint is broken and bent.

Bathe the wounds already **infected**,
  Cry for help too late interjected,
A broken bough of tree,
  That which now suspends me.

49.
THE SPIRIT OF THIS MAN

You spoke and everyone listened,
   "All stand!" in the court was heard,
Nothing I had done was any good it seemed,
   The **spirit** of this man may as well be dead.

How do you sleep at night?
   You redefine justice as blight,
You mock a father's right
   And **destroy** a daughter's sight.

You erode a sacrament,
   But it isn't to your detriment,
You amass a **swelling** fortune,
   Have you ever heard the evening loon?

To you it matters not
   What the fat bastards got,
To you it's **black** and **white**,
   You make me vomit as you smite.

So do fall and break your nose,
   Trip on those pretentious robes,
You're not **worthy** and should be dead,
   With half a chance, when all is said.

50.
BUSTED

Busted by the trusted,
    Toned not phoned,
Spat at by the fat,
    The jaws of the ex-in-laws.

Feeling, not reeling,
    Mousey, not housey,
A beer to make you queer,
    Sacred wine from the vine.

That shard runs deep and sharp,
    Harsh the sound from harp,
Melodic the tone,
    In this here zone.

Spoken and broken,
    Beaten, mistreating,
Help for the strangled shore,
    On the brow of our countries evermore.

Stumbled and fallen,
    To you I'm calling,
Who are you anyway?
    I know I can't say.

Another page from my desk falls,
   As I end up on all fours,
Drugged and drunk,
   You belong in a trunk.

The cut so deep,
   The pain did throb,
The sleep stolen,
   The dirty swab.

The limbs amputate,
   No way to repair,
My God, what a state,
   This life of despair.

The knife sunk in my heart,
   The broken bone apart,
Before this state did start,
   What was I then, smart?

This probably sounds so terribly smug,
   But it seems I'm the stupid mug,
Ebola, AIDS, bird flu, whatever the bug,
   That wipes out nations with just a shrug.

51.
COMPANIONS

My trusted companions of choice,
    A pen, paper and my voice,
My guitar, that reads my mind
    When **darkness** leaves me blind.

Breaking out of this cell,
    Upon many rocks I fell,
Can't say I believe anymore
    About that **opening** door.

I think the line is three score and ten,
    But to me two and ten is just fine then,
So, JAcOB wandered into my space
    And took a seat, to make it his **place**.

The reading of this work is clear,
    There's much to do here,
But my vision is obviously mere,
    Of the **work** to bring this near.

I want the common person to know,
    I want the beaten woman to show,
I want all the oppressed to be OK,
    Is that a **crime** to ask for this way?

For we ignore the demon at our peril,
   It lurks in the darkest dankest hole,
Ready to snap its baying jaws,
   And **drag** your soul with its claws.

They say that people in houses of glass
   Shouldn't throw stones as they pass,
They say do as you'd have done,
   And **resist** the urge to punch someone.

They say a woman is a princess,
   Treat her as such and not a bit less,
They say be true to yourself,
   Don't **chase** the glory or the wealth.

Many say if you have a buck,
   Give it away as a token of luck,
And should you happen to hear,
   Let my girls **know** I loved them so dear.

They say, of JAcOB, many folk,
   He's just an ordinary bloke,
Tried his utmost to do his best,
   Fell **short** and that was his test,

And of all the things I've heard,
   The bland, the rich, the plain, and absurd,
I can do nothing but leave these books,
   One day you can tell me **how it looks**.

52.
THE LINEN LANDSCAPE

The linen **landscape** of love's far reaches,
    Endless like the sand on Juno's beaches,
Telling the **stories** of love, lost and found,
    Yet it seems the wheel keeps going round.

And whosoever hears this **sound**,
    While these words spin around,
Will **stand** with me, to face God's wrath,
    Or be washed up in Hell's burnt chaff.

One might well argue about a slave to **rhythm**,
    The metering, the rhyming and syllable driven,
But I'll not be restrained by **opinion**,
    Like or not these words, that's your decision.

There's not much I look at these days
    That sends the **blues** on their strange ways,
Or that provokes a word of note,
    Not that I'm looking for an **approval** vote.

But the most inane of object
    Finds my pen, with some **subject**,
And I suppose it will end up somewhere,
    Probably **tangling** in an angel's hair

And yeah, go ahead and bring me to account,
    For all the **wrongs** and any amount
Of all the suffering my hands cause,
    And when I'm dead you can think, and **pause**.

The Ramblings of my Madness

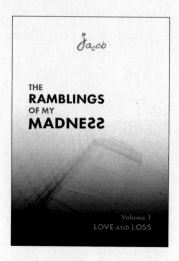

Volume 1 - Love and Loss

Volume 2 explores the love and loss in my life, as a result of depression, my own actions and the actions of others outside my control.

Released on May 1st 2015.

The Ramblings of my Madness

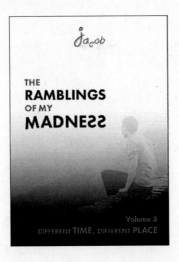

Volume 3 - Different Time, Different Place

Volume 3 enables me to explore the many different cultures that I've experienced and how this leads me to reflect upon things in a different way, dependent on where I might be and what I might be experiencing. I've been fortunate to travel, but each place brings a different perspective and interesting challenges.

Released on June 23rd 2015.